1

Butterfly Words

Butterfly Words

Zelda Black

@zeldablack_

Cover art by: K.A.P.

TRIGGER WARNING:

Topics such as:

- Mental illness

- Depression

- Suicide

- Alcoholism

- Trauma

- Death

And more will be mentioned throughout this book.

Please make sure to take care of yourself; if you need to take a break, please do. This was not easy to write; I can imagine it will not be easy to read.

Out of that pain and suffering…

came Butterfly Words

Contents

Blue tears

&

Broken hearts

T o my friends and family,

The reason I am writing my sadness from the past, not the present.

I'm bleeding out my feelings

Onto these pages

In hopes that you'll understand

I was cut by words

My skin turns pale

Much like this paper

At the brink of death

I think of you

You

You

You

You played your heart strings like a violin

A melancholy tune in an empty arena

Every day, you would be there

No applause

No crowd

Then your strings broke

You broke

Now everyone wants to see you

When it's too late

I consider home a place I'm not welcome

Singing and laughing with no attention

Taking the laughs over cries

And wiping the memory as if it were a stain tainting
your perfect record

You ask how I am, as if you cared

What can I say?

I'm living my best life

Hoping for it to end

I hate that you make me want to end me

There's just something comforting about sadness

Knowing at this point it can't be any harder than it is

now

When you asked me to let go of the past

You asked me to let go of *everything I have*

I'm not scared of nothing

I've had nothing before

It hurts less accepting this fate

Rather than crawling to the top

Just to be beaten down again

I'm admitting something that sickens me

I feel responsible for her death

Endless nights of begging her to talk to me, to let me in

She silenced herself and therefore she died in pain

My words meant nothing to her,

So why should they mean anything to you?

Desperately searching through my heart

I looked for the switch

Let me turn it off

I NEVER WANT TO FEEL AGAIN

You weren't the knight in shining armor the movies portrayed

You were beaten and battered from the war

Your tattered fabric barely held together

You were tired, I was tired

We were suffering all the same

There's no need for armor when the battle is inside

Neither of us was equipped with a sane mind

And I still live, wondering why you didn't

Love leads you into dangerous places

Keep your eyes open

And your heart closed

It's okay, I'm used to it
The abandonment
The notion of all good things must come to an end
Trust me, this feeling of rock bottom
Is far from foreign

It's the worst feeling, being a stranger in your own
skin

That constant feeling of never being welcome, even in
your own body

Begging and pleading the powers above

To wake up and see a completely different person

The constant urge to rip off your skin

And replace it with new parts

I have the power to stop my pain from growing

But I don't have the power to stop my pain from hurting

I do not fear the end

I fear the path that made the beginning

Please, be here to tell your story

The last thing I ever wanted

Was to tell it at your funeral

How I wish I could crawl out of my skin

And shed off all my sins

It gets lonely at midnight without your warmth

Luckily for me, cold isn't a foreign feeling

I yearn to feel clean

If water could wash our minds

Everyone would be fine

Cursed are the ones with sane minds

For they have to watch this world crumble

By the hands of the ignorant

As much as I resent her for stealing you from me

I can't stay mad at her forever

You didn't even love me enough to stay

So I guess it was never even stealing

Maybe you're right

Maybe I do like the pain

It's a subtle reminder

That I can still feel

I can't remember my life without the pain

If there was ever a time

I've accepted that I am destined to settle in it

I am not, nor was I ever, a good person

I have fed the flames of hell for far too long

This is penance

This is payback

For all that I have caused

That's the funny thing about peace

We all want it

We just have different perceptions on how to achieve
it

How come I want to hurt everyone

When the only person that truly hurt me

Is myself

Open arms lead to open wounds

Don't think I'll ever forgive you again

Such a dismal feeling

Wanting you to be happy

But watching you flourish without me

Is the exact thing that's killing me

I bleed words that tell a story

My scars narrate them in a hushed tone

You stole the stars in my eyes

And stopped the flutter in my heart

My fingers struggle to pry open my heart

I used to know what to say in situations like these

I used to know how to comfort

But I locked my heart and buried the key

Say something

Save them

They'll die if you don't

It isn't that I don't care

It's that I don't have any more energy to give

I am not responsible for your life

Just as I wasn't for your death

You said you didn't judge a book by its cover

But you ripped mine

And made it seem like I was damaged from the start

I've spilled my guts just to make you stay

I ripped myself apart just to put you back together

And you left

You *still* left

I gave you my beating heart

And you still used those pills to stop it

It was never enough, all of me

You were bound to break from my arms

Gone too soon

My soul is bound to skin and bones

Shoved into flesh

I want to be more than the mortal body I am contained
in

You were my favorite oversized sweater

You helped me hide parts of me I thought were worth concealing

You had a lingering scent of familiarity

I found comfort in hiding who I am

And you were more than happy to provide that

I thought you were what's best for me

But lies are far more comfortable than the truth

Comfort can be a twisted provider of relief

It doesn't do my heart justice simply knowing other
people care

I am not hurting because I think no one cares

I don't care

And that's what hurts the most

Three names are permanently embedded in my brain

One

Too many midnight pills

Two

An angel that wanted to go home

Three

Death got closer to you than I ever could

In sleepless nights I wonder

Was I the last straw?

Every time you took another pill

Every night your heart couldn't take it

Every night spent at the hospital

Did I even phase you?

I am walking on thin ice

The ice beneath me is fragile and cold

Delicate to the touch, it burns against the warmth of
my feet

Ever so carefully I tread looking ahead at the
unknown

Why do I tread?

Why do I persist when I know I will break and plunge
deep into the abyss?

Must I carry on?

I am still treading, living with my stomach in knots

And my heart clogging up my throat

The birds up above me glide elegantly across the sky

Up there they need not fear

How I long to be with them

I have not seen a light or a sign of any God

There is only so much the fragile ice can take

But I'll be damned if I am to sit here and wait for
death

Butterfly Words

They just fly out of my mouth

Without intentions of the consequences

In a cocoon the tension grows

The anger grows

Until it breaks

Until I break

I call them Butterfly Words

I feel so selfish

Wondering while you were on the brink of death

If I ever phased you

I just need to know I meant something

I need to know you cared about me too

Do you regret those pills?

Do you regret taking that drive?

Do you wish you were still here?

I'm paranoid now; I can't lose anyone else

All those years ago, I never could comprehend why
someone would end their life

And as I got older, *I wondered why I didn't*

Love isn't for people like us

We will always be the protector

Not the protected

We don't settle

This is our torture, our price

To have such beautiful gifts

That bring good and bad

But we must endure them alone

I'm always hurting the most

When I can't feel a damn thing

You left

But the memories of you still linger

You left and I became hollow

There are ghosts that roam in my once vibrant eyes

My bones creak as I tread to my lonely grave

I am not haunted

I am the haunting

And there is nothing left of me

The moon is a goddess

Raging war against the sun with an army of stars

She glistens against darkness

I want to be like the moon

Perhaps she was right, when she said the poet will always lust for misery

That love wasn't for the tortured artist

I only write when I'm in pain

The only part I love about me is my bones

The only part I don't wish to tear off and replace

Every part of me I want gone

It'll never end; the urge to look in the mirror and try
to find someone different

Yet it never happens

No God has come to save me from the torture I inflict
on myself

The hatred I can't erase

The complete vulgar disgust I have

I stole my smile and halted my laughter

Self-inflicted pain *I never fixed*

You painted the sky with your lies

And told me I could reach for the stars

How blissful it seemed

Before the truth seeped in

And what if I'm not strong enough?

To carry this heavy heart

Tidal waves come crashing into my soul

Ready to *sink* me

Ready to *kill* me

I just want my thoughts to leave me alone

Bile rises in my throat thinking of all the potential I'll
never have

How does one escape pain

When it's self-inflicted?

I'm wringing out my soul

And ripping out my hair

Any pain, any memory

To produce one more poem

Frost-bitten kisses

Are not enough warmth this time

The cold caresses our skin

Entwined in a frozen prison

Our love couldn't keep us warm

When will you realize

That your life was meant to be more

Than an eternity of regret?

Our love was the sunset

Beautiful

But only from a distance

I hate to see you walk away

When the booze strides in, claiming to stay

It's hard, *loving someone that's half present*

Oh, how we yearn to fly

When all we can do is taste the ground

You may not know it

But your silence was just as loud as her hate

Sometimes I wonder if I'll ever win this battle

Life against death

Will I be here today, will I lose?

I can't choose which side I'm on

Who am I fending for, what do I want to fight for?

Thus the battle rages on

And I scramble to pick a side

Will this sword pierce the enemy?

Or pierce me?

Or are we one in the same?

It has been centuries since I've tasted my own tears

This tragedy has brought me to my knees

For so long I have clawed my way up to a

smile

How do people laugh so effortlessly?

It takes everything I have

For so long I was happy

I've learned to never settle

Everything dies

When you least expect it

Like the harsh tug of the waves

She pulled you in

And kicked you out

In a toxic cycle of mental abuse

I always wondered if you'd be strong enough to break
from her current

I just hope you don't drown trying

With broken arms

I still hand you everything I have

My bones are begging me to withdraw

To stop

Heal myself for a change

But my heart refuses

I will always hand you everything I have

Even when you smack it to the ground

And laugh in my face

If only it were that simple

To wipe away that pain

Like spilt coffee on the ground

It's scraping the tears off your face

It's quieting the thousands of voices in your head

It's pressure on your chest when your lungs are just fine

And the pain is worse when you say

Get over it

Just like that, I was invisible again

Even when I worked

so hard

t o   b e   s e e n

I am fire

I am warm, inviting, comforting

I am exciting, passionate, and radiant

I am fire

I am dangerous, angry, and harmful

I am flammable, easily flared up

I am destruction

I am the reason you'll burn if you come too close

I am the reason you'll leave

"I miss you," she cried.

"I miss the person that you once were," I replied.

I'm starting to think nothing will ever be enough

You always work towards this constant goal

A never-ending pit of desire brewing within your heart

More, more, more

You say you'll stop then, but I don't think you will

It's a constant need of validation

From anyone but yourself

You heard, "I'm fine"

But you didn't see the inevitable death in her hollow
eyes

Sometimes what you can't see

Becomes the most visible

When you're too late

I miss you and everything I loved you for

But I wonder

Has a new person taken over?

Or have I fallen in love with the mask you created?

Alone is a word embedded in my mind here to stay

As I walk this narrow road of life I am left barefoot

Each step another bruise added to my aching feet

This would be less painful if I had a hand to hold

If I had a voice that said, "keep going"

I may be alone

But the loneliness is what has kept me company for so
long

I do not wish to have company that can break me

And step on the scattered pieces of who I once was

Alone is a word I am now comfortable with

This solitude has numbed my mind into thinking

This is okay

You must think I'm a puzzle

I'm still trying to pick up the pieces

I'm still trying to find them

You can't just break me

And expect me to fix myself again

Words held more promise for me

than voices ever could

Please

Hold my cold, withering hands

I sense I may not roam much longer

I have seen death and have died with it

With hollow eyes and an absent mind

I cannot keep hold of this mental bloodshed

There is no future for me

And there is no love in this life

She called me honey because I was sweet

Sweet was how she waltzed into my life with promises of the future

Sweet was how she roped me into her arms with gratitude

Sweet was how she used to be

Sweet coats the sour taste that must be swallowed

I could not swallow the fact that you were not as sweet as you claimed to be

I called her love

Because love isn't always as blissful as it seems

That smile you wore everyday

Was now reserved for special occasions

Shame on you for thinking you could live a life

With someone whose life has already started

How gifted we poets are, painting our stories with
words

Yet it seems we must bludgeon ourselves to near
death

To produce our most beautiful pieces

*How come our stories must always be written with
tears...*

When I see you it's as if the world stops

Everything seems to come to a halt

As I gaze upon those eyes

I want to tell you,

I love you

I love you

I love you

Until my lips fall off

I want to hold you

Until my hands go numb

I want to know everything about you

Until I know it all

But that's not my privilege to have, is it?

It's his

It doesn't do my heart justice simply knowing other
people care

I am not hurting because I think no one cares

I don't care

And that is what hurts the most

A withering mess of melancholy and gin

Are you ready to screw up again?

Passionate nights of lust and liquor

You live from sunup to witness sundown

Gallivanting across town from bar to bar

This is not the friend I knew

Which one are you truly after:

Other people's love and support

Or your own?

I hated her with every fiber of my being

"You're my worst enemy"

I said, *pointing to the mirror*

HELLO

IS

JUST

AS

BITTERSWEET

AS

GOODBYE

Your words were a pistol planted against my temple

And I told you to shoot

I'm sorry I'm the only one hurting

Upon realizing things aren't the same anymore

Love can blind us

And stop us from being who we are meant to be

But sometimes love can nourish us

And we grow into someone we never thought we
could be

Plant yourself around those who tend to you

You have confided in this ancient grief

Listened to its whispers for far too long

Don't let time waltz away from those cold, calloused hands

She was buried in the garden

Where his love grew like flowers

Love lived in the garden

And died in the mansion

Does love die?

She inquired softly

I replied,

Was love ever alive?

Have you ever wanted something so bad,

But you know in your heart what you want will neve
happen?

Yet still you persist

With bleeding hands and aching feet

Your mind implores you to stop

But you're too enticed by the possibilities

Of what was never meant to be

It's heart-wrenching to see how your smile never
shows

Your happiness was shoved in memories from long
ago

Then you became a memory, too

I wanted to talk about it

So I did

My pen cried with every syllable – every word

Sobbing ink into papers arms

I was an unstoppable storm

As feelings began to brew

Suddenly, I realized my pen was not the only one
crying

She had a kind of love that would cross horizons

It's a shame that ours wouldn't even cross paths

I'm trying to pick up the pieces of who I once was

And craft it into something beautiful

But like sand it slips from my grasp

F

A

L

L

I

N

G

Into the ever-growing darkness

Sometimes,

It takes a stronger person to walk away from the problem

That must be why you left

I was your problem...

You're like a hangnail

Festering your way into my flesh, hanging idly by

It pains me, so I try to pull you away

It hurts

Excruciating, stinging, unbearable pain

So I decide you can stay

But you loom over my presence more

The torturous sensation grows

When will I ever muster up the strength to get you out
of my life?

You know it is love

When you yearn to hold them

But bare the heartbreak of never having them

She wore her heart above her head

As if it were a crown

Love before everything else

She was so smitten with him

We start off young

When love is strong

Like an untamed flame

We remain enticed in eternal bliss

Will we ever wake up?

She was the kind of girl you wanted to know
everything about

With her brunette curls and forest green eyes

She drew you in and kicked you out

She was the kind of girl your arms reached out to, but
she never reached back

She was the kind of girl to say, "I love you" and never
truly show it

She was the kind of girl I met

She was the kind of girl that left

I am thinking

Of course it's about you, isn't it always?

I'm trying to graft skin over the wounds you inflicted

What if you came back?

What if you graced me with your presence and held
me tight

Like you used to do

Whispering sweetly how sorry you were

Would I give into your touch?

Or would I walk away?

The most painful moments

Make beautiful poems

In its own funny, fickle way

Pain is beauty

The caged bird sings

In a life of solitude

Bars of narrowed minds cage the individual

It longs to sing its carefree tune

The caged bird sings

Of a time it can use its wings again

It was the wind that caressed your features

It was the sun that kissed your skin

It was I that yearned to do these things

Yet it was he that said he could provide you with the world

But the world is not his to give

It was I that offered you my heart, time, and devotion

I offered you my world

Yet it was he who knelt down on one knee

It should have been me that was he

Alas, if you wanted it that way, you would've told him no

I used to come to you when I was upset

Now every time I see you, I am upset

Ironic how your sanctuary can burn into flames

And turn into the headache you strived to escape from

I stopped wearing makeup for that period of time

It got so bad to the point where I couldn't fix myself
with makeup

I could barely look at me

I was *disgusted* with me

My appearance used to be everything

Until I never wanted to see me again

I am like a stream, always in motion

If you looked past the murky waters you can see rocks

Sharp, jagged rocks

Though it seems I am steadily flowing

The rocks scrape and tarnish my skin

If you looked closer, you could see creatures dwelling within

Love, hate, anxiety, happiness

But you didn't

You only came to glance from a distance

I endure all of this with a steady flow

And all in peaceful silence

I cried an ocean, in hopes you'd drown

But it was I that had drowned

You kept safe with your feet by the shore

They dance and drink

So they never sink

Into their own emotions

Your words linger and always keep me hanging

Like a noose around my neck

How long must I hang

Before I give out?

It's not that I want to die

It's that I'm stuck with this constant feeling of sadness and regret

That makes me feel like I don't deserve the life I'm living

I have no idea where it comes from

I didn't ask for it

And the only words that can describe it are:

I want to die

EVERYTIME

      I reach, I keep bleeding

      But I'll continue to reach

NO MATTER

HOW MANY

TIMES

I

KEEP

BLEEDING

Why do you do it?

Jumping from girl to girl

Heart to heart

As if they were steppingstones towards some form of salvation

As if girls hearts were meant to be tally marks across your wall

As if it were a competition, a game you were set to win

Hearts are not yours to keep

Your tally marks will end here

She loves me

She loves me not

Those words spiral in my head

E V E R Y D A Y

Breaking off petals does not decide what becomes of
us

But I need some form of hope

t h a t   w e   s t i l l   h a v e   a   c h a n c e

My mind shouted,

I love you

But my lips fell silent

Nothing was said that day

Shakespeare once said love looks not with the eyes
but with the mind

Yet the beauty industry says otherwise

They'd rather a girl focus on how she looks to the eye

That she lose her mind in doing so

This time it was too late to patch the scars you've left
on my heart

You left a permanent mark on me that I can't shake

You can't kiss it away

You can't give me flowers to make me smile

This time, it can't be fixed

I was the fireplace to keep you warm

I wasn't enough, so you snuffed out the light in me

And moved onto something more

I could hear the rustling of the leaves

But I couldn't hear you calling my name

The harsh autumn breeze slapped my face

And brought me back to reality

The reality that you weren't even there

The whispering winds of Mother Nature beckoned me

The sun beams down on me

Surrounding me with the warmth you never provided

"Have you got a boyfriend yet?"

I hate questions

With a sheepish smile, I shook my head

"Boys will come begging to you one day, just you wait!"

I hid a frown,

I know, but I don't want them

A girl

And

A girl

Fall in love

You say it is toxic, it'll morph young minds into
becoming homosexual

As if it were a disease

A boy

And

A girl

Fall in love

You say it's beautiful, charming and cute

Love

Is

Love

If I had known that, I would've come to terms with
who I am years ago

When it grows cold and you're sitting by the fire

Don't forget my embrace was warmer

When he embraces you in his arms

Remember I held you tighter

When he knelt down on one knee

Remember how I knelt under all the pressure to make
you smile

You forgot all too easy

I suppose it was the blinding shimmer of that diamond

That also blinded your heart

You've beaten me senseless

I am numb

Numb to your punch

But also to one's touch

Words of endearment, compliments, and praises don'
phase me anymore

Neither do your tantrums, ill terms protruding from
your mouth

Words fade, like you soon will

I'd rather feel nothing

Than fall for your words again

The saddest part is

I don't miss you

Because I never knew what it was like having you

You know you've become hollow

When tearing others down

Is the only thing that lifts you up

I have to sink into the reality that you're going away

But I can't sink any deeper

When I'm already drowning

I called you weak for giving your heart to the one you love

Until I realized it's painful

Prying out your heart

Entrusting it in someone else's hands

Many times I've looked in the mirror

And tried to see what all the boys find so attractive

But I've looked harder

To see what the girls don't see

Every form fitting outfit

Every lipstick

I've tried too hard

And end up with nothing, but a silent reply of,

"Why can't you just be straight?"

In the vast sea of galaxies

We were blessed with eternal beauty

Yet when I gazed upon him

He had those same melancholy optics

I saw the ocean in his eyes

If only I had stopped admiring his oceans

And leaped in to save him

From the same exact beauty that was drowning him

Vengeance with a silver tongue

T o those who tried to break me,

Well, at least you tried.

I won't fight battles for someone that won't stay by
my side

I won't get cut

For someone that's cut me

You expect me to lift my sword in your name

When your name is what plagues me at night

Sickens me to the core

I'm fighting my own battle

Against you

I have my own sword

Forged by your blood, sweat, and tears

I'll engrave my own name

By killing yours

Nevertheless, I tread into the dark

And let the forest consume me

Bury my corpse in leaves

And engulf me in vine

I'll be waiting for you, *half past nine*

I crumble at the cold that bites my wings

And tears at my skull

When God said he'd cast me into the flames of sin

Little did he know I was born of fire

You can't kill me *with what fuels me*

I hope you found peace in abandoning me,

I hope you know I'm not cold without your absence

Your arms were keeping my weak heart warm

But once you trashed it aside

I learned to conjure my own eternal flame

Of *hell*

I'll bury you in my mind and bruise your ego

I'll slither my way into your darkest secrets

Slit open your mind

You

Will

Die

Like

I

Have

I am the darkest clouds looming over your head

I am the chill that crawls up your spine seeping into your darkest thoughts

I am not the henchman bringing death

I bring life

I bring the kind of life that tears at the seams of sanity

I bring the kind of life that makes perishing a bliss

You cannot get rid of me because I exist inside you

Go on ahead, reach inside and try to pry me out

I'm in your head now

And there is no ending me

A piercing cry awoke the night

My eyes are bleeding words, my smile coated in
barbed wire

I am desolate

There is no monster within the man

There is monster that is man

It's that yearning feeling, isn't it?

The satisfying crunch of her skull against your heels

Brushing the dust of her bones off your blouse

And tasting a fresh kill

How different you are, *once the sun goes down*

The soft skin your hands loved to grasp turned
callused

The smile you insisted I provide turned jagged

You tried to mold me into yours

Turns out you molded me into the monster you feared

Ten years old, they were already hurling their words at me

Taunting the way my nose didn't quite match my
features

I wasn't appealing to them

Their words echoed in my head throughout the day

They'd approach me in packs like wolves, ready to
feast on dinner

Because to them I was

Feasting on my agony, how do I taste?

Are my tears too salty for you?

How about the cuts from your claws forged by nasty
words, are you done yet?

My blood boils, anger coursed through my veins

I was never one to bite as they have bitten me

You were seething with rage so much

That you were drowning in it

Suffocating in the fire you bred

I could see you were on another rage fit

Anger was the mistress that coaxed you

Into another boozed-filled night

Every punch to the mirror

Scattered blades of glass coated with blood

It was just another night for you

Running wild in red shoes

I always keep Satan on his toes

He can barely keep up with the things I do

Starting off with me and you

What was meant to be happily ever after

Turned into a straight up disaster

Kiss your life goodbye

You better be prepared to *die*

Your optics suddenly flickered into innocence

You had realized what you'd done

And with a small voice you asked me for forgiveness

Bruised and battered, I was ready to open my door

But I replied,

"No. It's time you ask *me* for forgiveness."

I've been hiding for far too long

I'm famished, I'm starved

In my cave I sit, yearning

For the blood of an angel

Scattered feathers from heaven's kingdom reside at
my grave

Are you ready to let me out?

It was cold in the absence of your embrace

You left me for dead

Malnourished and starved for affection

I was my own helping hand

I learned how to live

Lift your wings

And show them how much *hell* an angel can raise

With creaking bones

A sour heart

And a twisted, pitiful smile

I ask the entity that calls itself a God,

"What am I here for?"

Pray all you like

It'll do you no good

When the streets are plagued with silence

And death sweeps brutally into homes

Taking young, taking old

I'm in your head, I've been here for a while

You opened the red door

And let him in

Do not mistake my shattered self

For a graveyard of what I once was

These shards of glass are my swords

Fighting for the life I want to live

It seems no matter how hard I fight to stay on top

The closest I'll be is second

There will always be someone prettier, someone more talented

It isn't fair, having to self-loathe every night

While others drift off into mindless slumber

I need others to taste what I have endured for so many years

I've become desperate enough to turn to revenge

So be it

The most dangerous thing

Is a woman with *murderous intent*

The end is near, can you feel it?

Satan's claws inching up everyone's back

Piercing their minds

This crooked world is just the beginning

You used to shiver in your sleep

You're in a coffin now, buried dark and deep

I kicked your grave with merciless eyes

"That's the thing about darkness:

You drown in it

O R Y O U

B E C O M E

I T"

Whenever I was able to stand, you shot me down

My face has hit the ground so much I can taste defeat

You want me to dwell down below where I belong?

Fine, I'll sink

Sink into your skin at your most vulnerable moments

Claw my way into your heart

I'll take your greatest weapon and make it mine

A new era

A new constitution scripted from your blood, sealed
with tears

Everything you said, I'll say it back

I'll bruise your heart with my silver tongue

I'll gouge your eyes out

Look what I've become

*YOU STARTED THE **FIRE** IN ME*

GOOD LUCK

PUTTING IT OUT

153

My body is a blank canvas and I am the artist

Each work of art is a piece of me made into something better than before

It is accepted to admire paintings on a wall but not on skin

People with tattoos do not go to hell

But condescending people do

You left your happiness to rot and die

Dust piles over the memories

Memories of the better you

Look at all you've left behind

To become the empty person you are today

And when it was my turn

To claim the throne

To sit and feast on what I've yearned for

I only thought of how it must feel

To be down below

In the dark, desolate wasteland

Grabbing at scraps, pleading for life

Greed had hold of me

Because being here

Never felt so good

I'm torn between two lives

The life of an angel

The depths of a demon

I can't choose

I can't pick sides

When two halves make a whole

I'll always be both

If we plead with our voices we'll never be heard

So we take to the streets, we break what we can

And shout out loud

We speak with violence because it is the only tongue
man will ever know

And it's about time we learn how to converse

When it gets dark, I don't fear the monsters that supposedly hide under my bed

I fear the dark thoughts that are stuck in my head

The storm that resides in me isn't what scares me

The urge to cower to darkness

The yearning to become it

What scares me is that it doesn't frighten me at all

It's rather enticing

They told me I'd never be Queen

So I crafted my own kingdom

Out of skin and bones

With swords for teeth, I flashed my killer smile

I am not only the Queen

I am the kingdom

T R Y

T O

T E A R

M E

D O W N

Society is much like clay

Eventually, everyone molds into the same thing

Sometimes I want to say I'm sorry

I'm a tough clay to mold

The evident whispers, narrowed eyes and stares

All try to mold me into what they are

I am not clay

I am stone

And you'll *bleed* if you try to mold stone

The flames of hell kiss each other every night

Satan has my soul

I'll never be one of those angels

Walking amongst men

Every memory of you I have

I want to hold in my hand

And crush it

I want to see it diminish

I want to see every memory of you

GONE

I was worried you'd stab me in the back,

Little did I know I should've kept my head
forward instead of behind

You're not as merciful as most

You aimed straight for my heart

And smiled as the blade seeped into my skin

I will have vengeance

Black thorns pierce your skin

A tangled mess of bourbon and sin

It's not called anger

It's called rationality

Is it so wrong if I turn the tables?

Is it considered wrong, if I turned things a little darker?

If I sat on your throne

And ordered the guillotine to come crashing down

Is it so wrong to drink from the salvation revenge offers?

Is it wrong being consumed by the intoxicating fumes of hatred...?

It fuels me

Ignites me

In ways hope never could

My energy derives from the pain you once caused me

Nothing felt better with roles reversed

Funny, you said I didn't have the guts to pull the
trigger

Honey, you're talking to the woman that walks
through fire

And bathes in the enemies' blood

Tell me, how did it feel?

To taste the tears of your own kin

To flash your teeth, barking transphobic slurs

Shutting your own flesh and blood out in the cold

Mother dearest

Lost her child over a dress

How much longer must we cry for justice, as another
innocent life is killed?

How long must tears run?

We will keep fighting, with every bone in our body

Justice is a hunger that lived in my ancestors before
me

We speak with violence

Because that is the only tongue man will ever know

The darkness

Oh, how it held me

Oh, how it coaxed me

To venture deeper into the unknown

The dark I feared all my life

But nothing felt better than being in its embrace

Trapped or enlightened?

Have I fallen victim to the depths or have I found the
strength to conquer it all?

When the fault cracks

When the ice melts

We read papers with blindfolds

Money can't stop the bodies from piling up

The stench of defeat ripe in the air

As we all prepare ourselves for a well-deserved
punishment

Money can't stop the irreversible damage we have
caused

The children crying for justice

The adults crying for silence

How fickle we are; we ravage this Earth killing
everything

Including our own kind

And have the audacity to call ourselves victims

This is what it looks like

When lovers die side by side

Bodies intertwined

Hand in hand

Together they stood, together they fell

Stumbling down deep into hell

Where they will endure their wrong doings

And burn

Just like the rest of us

I tried being nice, but look at all it has cost me

So I turned the page to a new chapter

And made things a little *darker*

It was an evident storm brewing

We all saw the signs and symptoms

My blood was boiling

And my teeth clenched

You ruined me

Now it was time for revenge

They call revenge bittersweet;

Something that doesn't roll off the tongue as easily

To me it's my sweet melody

A craving that has no satisfaction

A never-ending thirst

For something beyond my potential

Storms protruding from her mouth

And blood stains on her lips

This is no era of damsels in distress

Long may she reign

You told me to never take shit from anyone

Yet you open yourself up like a doormat

And everyone steps on you

Perplexed and angered,

What do I do?

You don't practice what you preach

You tell me to be better

Yet you should do the same

He lifted his sword in God's name

Wielding his blood-soaked Bible

Claiming to know peace

There is blood on him

There is blood on everyone

He holds his hands in prayer

And claims to know God

His hands in prayer morph into fists

Beating down those who oppose him

He claims to be kind

Only to those on his side

He claims, he claims, he claims

It didn't matter what he said

When the rebellion hung him

Leaving him for dead

A part of me would give anything to roll back time

Yet another part of me understands this pain was long
overdue

We'd buried our heads in the sand and called it peace

It hurts now to confront what we ignored centuries
ago

But we must push forward

Right our wrongs

And kill the king on his throne

You taught me to sit and wait for a man

But I am not a princess

I am a dragon

A towering, malicious, deceiving beast

With a growl, I make men tremble

I breathe the fire that will burn them

down

Whoever said being the villain wasn't fun?

Bury me six feet under

I will rise ten feet above

You'll never see me; it's all in your head now

The smallest crevasses in your heart is where I reside now

Making it hollow, emptying it out

I should've known; I can't hurt you on the outside

You'll die on the inside, *just like I have*

You like the bottle more than me

You like getting so plastered it clouds your judgement

You like the craving, the buzz

Lapping up each ounce of beer, tequila, whiskey

Name any liquor, you consume it

You like the bottle more than your friends

You like the haziness of waking up next morning

Better than making nights to remember

You don't like the bottle, you love it

I don't like to forgive

It invites opportunity to hurt me again

And then I can only blame me when you choose to do
so

I don't like to inflict pain

But if you hurt me, I'll make you bleed

Death has to take

In order for life to give

Funny, *how it doesn't even phase me*

Oh, how I loved someone's blood on my hands

To scratch the itch

To tame my hunger

Dowse the fire within

All went quiet

The day I died

The cicadas snicker at night

As they lurk in the field

He's calling my name

He sneaks into my brain and dances around my skull

Giving me thoughts

Giving me wonders

It's scary to know

That this mind is occupied by two

You said I wasn't dark enough to go down the road of
revenge

My dear, I paved that path centuries ago

I'll use my talons to drag your lifeless corpse

Right down to hell with me

Because if I'm going down

I will most certainly go accompanied

Entitled, selfish vultures

You are the toxic poison seeping into this world's
veins

Your God will abandon you

In order to save itself

You are a beam of light enticed by darkness

Dancing with shadows and holding stars

Crawling into the darkest of corners

You grow weary of your normal life

And strive to fight what you're so against

Be careful of that darkness

The same one you fight

Could consume you in a second

Sometimes we become the very thing we sought to destroy

What has the light done for you?

Come to the darkness where we reside

Even to the purest of souls

Nothing compares to the comfort darkness brings

You'll sink into it just as I have

You'll fight it at first, as most do

Pray to your false God

Slam your palms together, begging for salvation

All mortals are dark at heart

Bred from greed, your God will abandon you

Are you worth saving?

And do you really want to be saved?

Watch me carve you out into an empty void

Watch me make you *bleed*

You didn't just break me, you broke what was left of me

You shattered all the mercy I had for you

I am not green with envy, I am red with hate

It just snapped, much like your neck

I am beyond repair

As are you

I'll drag you down to hell with me

And we'll both bathe in the flames of our sins

I told you I'd never let you go

The Grieving

I once saw a white horse

Its blood-shot eyes, full of remorse

I closed my eyes, praying it away

Dear Lord, give me pain another day

Take thy blade, sharp and silver

Death is what I shall deliver

To all who woe

For a good soul

Goodbye, baby, I'll see you in another life

Perhaps once or twice

I'm sorry I lost you

I just couldn't pull through

You could've been in my arms

Instead you're giving yourself scars

Goodbye, baby, perhaps one day you'll know

That the child, lonely and small

Was mine

I had one mission

To change your vision

Make you see that it's me

The one you could've called daughter

Alas, I was sent to the slaughter

I talk to people that are dead

They know what I have to dread

One day you'll know the child you lost

Found you

I once saw a red door

But it was so much more

I didn't know what it was for

It is no ordinary door

Blood stained wood

Wounds from the good

As warriors they stood

Alas, they fell

Now they descend into hell

Shiny silver knob

I can hear a faint sob

Silver tears fall

Here, evil stands tall

Enter if you dare

But if you must, beware

That red door is not what you're looking for

Nothing to eat, nothing to do

Better just let them eat my bones through

Sins, they're out for the kill

Sins, they feed on the thrill

Burning hell

My sanity, caught in a well

Staring at the light, day by day

As I wait for my sins to rot away

You may not have killed him

But the words you threw at him

The constant hatred protruding from your mouth

Held the gun to his head

And told him to shoot

Alms for the poor, alms for the poor

Please ma'am, can't you spare one more?

Greed in our veins and death in our heart

Let's use our blood as our art

Poisoned churches and soulless searches

We are the generation of today

Empty promises, broken lies

I will carve out your eyes

The city of ash will fall with one big smash

Blood red skies, echoes of twisted cries

Dirt on our faces, we don't belong in these places

Alms, alms in the city of ash

In the city of ruin

I hear these words in my head

How I wish I were dead

I'll hang myself up by a tree

Night and day, to try and scrape the pain

away

Opened my eyes and heard the cries

Endless lies, who really tries?

Try to end myself everyday

I just won't go away

Oh, resurrection, my life isn't perfection

Life gets tiring, hearing all the sighing

I wake up every day, pain sticks like glue

I'm young, I'm having no fun

No wrinkles, no special moments

Oh, agony... oh, resurrection

Today I'm going to plant a tree

In the middle of winter

Cold and damp outside

Perfect, perfect weather

Today I'm going to plant a tree

Out in the open cold

Just to watch my hope bloom then burn

Go ahead and call me insane

I just wanted to feel the pain

Another night

Drowning in the freezing rain

There is a story

A very scary story

Older than time, a tale that is mine

There once was a girl that saw demons

They visited her every night

Oh, how they gave her a fright

Now that she's older her bones break

All this pain she can't take

Bright yellow eyes, claws of such unreal size

Demons, demons that haunt her head

How she wishes she was dead

Keep popping the pills, it's not what really kills

It's the demons inside your head

Don't close your eyes, don't bleed tonight

I heard the demons coming

And they're coming for you

Isolation, isolation

Takes a toll on us all

Walls closing in, we slowly begin to fall

No more pleasant new faces

No more spreading our cultures

These fools, those vile vultures

Isolation, isolation

All we need is to build up our greed

We're all bleeding, in the sense of needing

Something new, something different

On the outside we stand tall and alone

A community of lies, through the walls you can hear cries

Cries of young, cries of old

Tough armor for skin, we will win

Hail the ruler, his soul growing colder

One, two, three, how long is it going to be?

Ethnocentrism in our heart, blood for our art

Take a drink, take a drink

As she gives you that seductive wink

Can't you see? This isn't meant to be

Hold a knife, hold a knife, are you willing to pay the price?

Am I too late? Why do I care?

You had an affair

You're rich, she's not

Can't you see her tie the knot?

Poison in your head, you foolish man

Now you are dead

She won

But hell, we aren't done

I'll smash the chandeliers, bring out her biggest fears

She was just a sinner

Now I am the winner

Poison, poison

I can feel the thorns, I see the devil's horns

Sad and angry

I'll put up a fight maybe

I'm ready to see the light

But have I enough energy to put up a fight?

Don't look away

Don't waste another day

Yes, your sins were bad

Sometimes it makes you think: do I deserve to be this sad?

Run through the thorns

Don't let them see your devil horns

Run to the light

And give it all your might

I'm ready to shut you out

Don't give me that pout

I've cried over you, what else was I supposed to do?

I'm tired of caring

I wish death is what you were wearing

I've been replaced

It was us you've disgraced

I'm ready to shut you out

You drunken fool

You worn out tool

You're not a child

But you're still reckless and wild

I wish you dead, yet I cling to this small thread

I still care, even with all this dread

But alas, sometimes you have to let go

Of the lover you've come to know

It seems day by day

You continue to slip away

At school I try to hide my grief inside

Young eyes gaze into old

Gentle and still, giving this world a chill

The disease kills you from the inside out

The children begin to pout, "Where's Mommy?
Where is she?"

Looking into the eyes of the young

The disease that has won

What to say, should I wait till the next day?

What a tragedy indeed

To see a family so displeased

With hearts slowly becoming undone

I live on a house over the hill

Fine, enter if you will

Twisted trees and buzzing bees

By the ocean, making all this commotion

We all died this very night

But you don't have to fright

We will kill you tonight

Use your bones as strings

And many more things

Carve out your eyes

Watching as the other sides

Rip out your hair, so silky and fair

I live on a house over the hill

Please, enter if you will

Poisoned apples, fun and games

Here lies the woman that prays

On her man's strength and love

Small, soft, a gentle dove

Sun-kissed blisters

From the woman that whimpers

Her man, not so loving as he once was

Yet she loves the monster she sees

The low scream from her lips

Turned into a forbidden kiss

Torture, pain

Greed is all we gain

She is still who she blames

Redemption for the Queen

To everyone that's stayed

This is for you; I hope you are proud

Funny, I act like I have everything to lose

In reality, I don't

That just means I have everything to gain

Sometimes I need to confide in others' words

Have them be a crutch I can lean on

To know that within my words lies a tale not just from me

But from someone else, too

I've always loved writing because it is the one thing
that is infinite

Feelings fade, people change, and friendships die

Even long after my death

These words will still remain somewhere

I guess you could say I strive to be infinite

Dear me,

It is vital for you to know

I do not blame you for his death

I do not blame you for not making him smile

I do not blame you

The only company I have is the girl in the mirror

And she's not much company

She doesn't laugh at my jokes like you do

Her eyes don't sparkle like yours do

Often times she's silent because she has nothing to say

If you can't handle the girl in the mirror

If you can't handle the awkward and distant me

With regret pooling in my eyes as I ready myself

For another midnight meltdown

Then you don't deserve the other side of me

The side that gets bruised but conceals it with a smile

You don't deserve the smile I give when I don't feel like smiling

You don't deserve the effort I put into making every day better than the last

We must all face our mirrors

She isn't ideal, but she's a part of me

If you're tired of the

WORLD

Look at it from a

DIFFERENT PERSPECTIVE

It was hidden in the unwanted silence

Your lingering caramel orbs and flushed cheeks

Lips slightly parted

We both said hello

Little we knew of what the future held for us

I'm glad I met you

A hero is not someone who saves everyone

But teaches everyone to save themselves

I place flowers on the grave of my past

My journey was hard, my journey was long

I don't like who I once was

But I love who I now am

But out of all this hate and division

Do you see the unity?

The power of everyone drowning the streets with their speeches

This will be written in history books

For the next generation's eyes to gaze upon

Take what you will from this moment

And learn from it

Your strength derives from peace

Not from anger

Too often do people mistake vengeance for strength

And that is why the arrogant fall

This is not your fight to lead

But to follow

To learn and absorb all you can

You can't lead a fight you haven't been hurt from

We always want to lead

Yet underestimate how powerful it is to follow

Strolling through memory lane isn't as leisurely as I'd like it to be

The roads are long, narrow cobblestone trails that lead to a desolate home

I have suffered long enough, enduring the pain of what I once was

I was living my life on repeat

I am no longer living on memory lane

I have moved on *and so should you*

The universe is capable of many things

It can guide you

Serve you

Shift your life

But it cannot grab your hands

And carve your own destiny

For that is up to you

Her words lifted me up

And gave me strength to be who I am today

I've abandoned my tears and enveloped my fears

Your words saved me, *now let me save you*

Breathless, I asked fate; *Who is she?*

Fate let me get to know her

I asked fate; *Let me see her again*

We met the next day

I asked my last question: *Is she the one?*

Tricky question; fate is still silent

They treat you as fragile not because you are

Because they know at your core

YOU

ARE

STRONGER

THAN

ALL

OF

THEM

Honey, you are more than the pain

It may be a cold night

But the sun will always rise

Into a new morning

I don't want to be loved by someone

I want to be loved by me

At times I must remind myself I am not here to stand
in front of you

I am here to stand with you

No one sprouts from jealousy

And when you tell me you love me,

I always want you to say it

As

If

It

Were

The

Very

FIRST TIME

Often times I dream of thriving off of revenge

Shoving my success in everyone who wronged me

But we do not succeed out of spite

We succeed to better ourselves

It isn't growth when you sprout from other's anger

When I gazed into your eyes

I saw my past

My present

And my future

That's when I knew

You'd be my world

I'm breaking open old wounds to find new beginnings

In my past there is the present

Somewhere in these dark depths of what I used to be
is a place for me to grow

I'm crawling through hell to find pieces of my old
misery

And turn it into another page

I hate my past, but I'll be damned if I went through
the pain for nothing

The light knows not of her name

She emanates such a profound and superior light

It degraded all that was once a God

Her presence lights up the room

Even the darkest of corners

She waltzed her way into my heart

I was captivated by her beauty

I

AM

ALL

YOU

SAID

I'D

NEVER

BECOME

You don't have to go *OVER*

THE

MOON

To capture my heart.

You just have to go

U N D E R

T H E

S E A

You're the sun that warms everyone in her presence

I am the moon, distant and cold

Yet somehow, opposites attract

We're a strange mix, but a perfect match

Somehow, you saw my rage as energy

You saw my tears as an opportunity for an outlet

You saw me as art

You took broken pieces and made a new puzzle

For that, I am eternally grateful

To the woman I love,

You're lucky; most of my material has stemmed from our experiences

I'm unlucky, you don't even know I love you

I used to suffer from my heartbreak

But look at all I've done with it

She is starlight

She is warm summer breeze brushing gently across
skin

She is the gentle touch of silk

She is the woman I love

Mountains coated in green

With waters blue

I knew I was home

As soon

As my eyes

F E L L

U P O N

Y O U

Not even the prettiest views

With the clearest skies

Can change the way I feel

When I look into your eyes

She's chasing the stars that beckon her name

And when she felt it, nothing ever felt the same

Sparkles pulsated through her veins

A vast sea of galaxies

She was ready for another journey

My scars are memories of who I was

And all I've overcome

Failure hurt me

And left permanent marks embedded in my skin

They're not flaws

They're reminders

Of all I've overcome

I find that my greatest exploration is in the
simplicities of where I dwell

Yes, there's a world out there, and in time I will see it

For now, *I want to be right where I am*

New rule:

If you don't give a shit about me, don't pretend you
do.

I only want the real people I deserve in my life

You only called me when you wanted something

Why must the beautiful things in life sprout from tragedy?

Why must love grow with heartbreak?

We take the good and we take the bad

It's the balance of life

The outcome of it all depends on your view

Which will you tend to more?

Will you choose to gain anything from your tears or simply wait for more to produce?

I am not the darkness you once thought I was

I'm not as broken over you as you thought I was

I have sprouted with the warmth and love surrounding
me

I have grown

I'm *over* you

I fell out of love

Into what seemed to be a dark hole

My life felt bland, an empty sheet

But life for me was not over

This time, life was actually for me

Mother Nature's guiding hands took me to the pen
and paper,

"Write all that you have felt"

I regret every moment I have spent seeking approval
of others

I regret trying to alter myself to appease them

It is wasted time and energy trying to be like everyone
else

You can't live a lie for your life

You are meant for *so much more*

At four years old I held a rose

I was unaware of the thorns piercing my skin

Causing droplets of blood to stain the floor

My Mother rushed to my side and told me to let go

I frowned and replied, "But it's so beautiful"

And she replied with, "No matter how beautiful, you
must let go of what hurts you"

Auburn curls set aflame

Captivated in pools of crystal blue

She sung her heart out of what she's gone through

I heard my story in hers

I knew we would connect

The best kind of people

Are the ones that pave their own paths

Straying from *normality*

To create *vitality*

WORDS SAVE LIVES

Never underestimate what good can come from bad

It doesn't hurt as much knowing you're not the only
one feeling this way

Be grateful you can endure the storm

Some people crave to know what it's like to walk
through the rain

And witness the other side

It isn't ours to decide where we are and what we may
face

Whether it be facing the sea or mountains

We are destined to be here

To conquer our demons

And tell our story

Nothing warms my heart more

Than knowing in my broken home

I am not alone

These tears have fallen plenty of times before

And hearts have healed

Remember me not by face but my name

Draw me as a towering tree

Up on a hill with an undisturbed view

With thickly embedded roots clinging to the ground

And though withered by cold nights my roots remain
unmoved

As the sun sets, providing a warm hue

I will stand still on my hill

With a blissful, undisturbed view

I dance with the storm

Learn to smile in the rain

And cry in the sun

I'm sorry it hurts

I'm sorry you may not understand

This uprising was written in the stars

I refuse to see this as tragedy

Look at the streets

What will you choose to see?

The rubble, the destruction

Or the people

Of all colors

Of all walks of life

Looking injustice in the eye

And demanding to right wrongs that have been
ignored

For centuries

There is more to me than sleepless nights and
midnight tears

There is heart flutters

And midnight laughs

Tears of laughter replace tears of pain

My journey has been long

And I have finally made peace

I am home

Her past was no

Glistening mansion

But her present could be

Some days are tough

There's always a little rain with the sun

But sit back and take a deep breath

A rainbow is somewhere

You have reached your destination

Why fret about the journey?

I have been empty and void of feeling for so long

It was all I had wanted to be

But then you came along

And made me want to be something more than hollow

I think I'm in love with you

Your feelings are not a burden

There's no need to build a wall

Let love pour into your heart

And let it flourish as if it were infinite

Pain is easy

It's easier to go downhill than up

It's tougher to find the light

Downhill doesn't have anything to offer

Your journey uphill may not be as easy as others

But persist, keep going

You will be met with a view

That will make you say,

I'm glad I kept going

Don't focus your attention to the parts that broke

The shards of smiles scattered across the floor

Look at the parts of me that stayed

That were brave enough to cling to my soul

What's scattered is gone

I'm human but I'm also strong

I promise I'm okay

I don't ever want you to think I'm a clean slate of silk
sheets

Glistening against the sun

We tend to display the best part of ourselves

And keep the remains of our pain scattered underneath
our bed

Show me your pain

Pain speaks more volumes than pleasure

This, this is why you stay

To throw your graduation cap in the air

To go shopping with your friends

To cuddle with your pets

To catch up with old friends

To look the love of your life in the eyes as you say "I
do"

To witness new beginnings you never thought you'd
see

This is why you stay

Please stay

I promise it's worth it

If life waited for convenience

We would never meet a challenge

There is an endless story

In those emerald green eyes

Let me read every chapter of you

Love is when I find myself wanting to run but wanting
to stare

I mustn't get too close

I drown at the sight of women like you

I never knew I could get so lost

In someone who's right in front of me

Her mind was a vast sea

Her soul, hiding the shipwreck of her past in the depths of her ocean optics

Any bold sailor would come to her

Claiming they could control her currents

They'd surely perish beneath her

She was self-destructive and often lost

Much like the sea, *there was too much of her*

Venture into the forest that is my mind

It is restless and wild

There is *life* within me

There is *power* within me

But that's the thing about good people

Even when they're handed nothing

While the evil run off with something

They still hold onto their morals

And never turn sideways into greed

That's what makes them good people

It is wasted energy

Crawling back to those

Who were never there in the first place

This awakening is like being enveloped in warm silk
sheets

Only to have the covers ripped off

Sometimes I wish I could crawl back into those sheets

And bury myself in good times

It's uncomfortable stepping into the light of truth and
justice

Using my voice is a newfound strength

It hurts to see the true aura of those around me

And as much as comfort beckons me

I refuse to be comfortable

I refuse peace

Until there is justice

Pain is much like a tree

It has roots, it stemmed from somewhere

But it's up to you, will you let it flourish?

Sometimes it's okay to let things die

If you're not thrown to the wolves

How will you ever learn to run with them?

How strong she is

To look at the rubble

And still find the happiness she so deserved

Some of the best things

IN

LIFE

Are pieced together after the

H E A R T B R E A K

Don't let it sadden you that your childhoods a ghost tow

Sometimes it's okay to let things die

Memories are often sugar coated and we forget the pain

But that pain paved our path to all we have now

There can be happiness even in suffering

The stars in your eyes shine a lot brighter

When you remember how hard you worked to achieve this

The bonds we mend overtime can wear and tear

Don't clutch onto what is wilting away

Keep searching for that spark you felt in the beginning

There is a lot more to life than settling

Once this is out in the open

Don't treat me like I'm fragile

Yes, I've had my times when I felt as if I were to
break

I've had my time to isolate; I've had my time to heal

I struggle much like the rest of us

The years have not been kind

I have healed and left those dark days behind me

Living without you is bitter

Bitter to not see you graduate

To not be at your wedding

To not hold you in my arms for the first time

I am healing

I am no longer keeping you a secret

I am ready to accept my pain and move on

I was alive, but I'm ready to live

Not even an ocean could hold all the regrets I have

But each one has led me to somewhere I never thought I'd be

Sometimes mistakes are a push in the right direction

The cold crisp wind blows

The leaves confide in the trees

Can you hear nature?

"Where do you think you're going?" Death roared, and I turned to face him with a smile.

"Forward."

Pain is temporary

It comes and goes like tidal waves

All you can do is keep your head above water

Destiny is a twisted blade

Wielded by a knight with no name

His armor tainted with the past

And when that day arrives

When you face him

Will you die by his blade?

Or will you make it your own?

If you can't appreciate the progress you've made

You'll never accept the finished project

Why settle for dirt on the ground

When there are stars in the sky?

You could do so much better

Than a man that wants your world

To be the palm of his hand

It's a constant balance of black and white

Love can thrive, love can die

We often think we must master life

And have the biggest houses or make the most cash

What we have to master is ourselves

That is what we have all forgotten

She traced her fingers over my scars

The ones I tried so desperately to bury

Under layers of clothing

She made me appreciate them

And all their former glory

Failure is not as dooming as it seems

It is a reminder

To appreciate all you've done to be where you are

Like an unfinished puzzle, your embrace didn't feel the same anymore

We didn't fit anymore

When I didn't find comfort in your arms

I found comfort in her voice

You said everything will be okay

She said it's okay to not be okay

She helped me grow

From people like you

Your eyes sparked a fire in my heart

Amongst the dark I could finally see

I am meant to be loved

The darkness will not kill me

Let these pages be the temple for your sanity

Please keep going

Everyone was born to have their own happy ending

That's when I realized I didn't want to be loved for
the way I looked

I wanted to be loved for the way I spoke

Every syllable, every word, I want to seep into your
heart and weaken your walls

I want to be the reason you open up and be the better
you

And that's when I decided

I want to show my scars too

I think I'm brave enough to publish this book

Have eyes, familiar and new, study my words

Find comfort, find fear, find love

I've had them hidden for so long

These words, these poems

Contain riddles of my life

I'm scraping the dust off my fears

And ready to bring them into light

To those who confide in my words

I am truly grateful to know on some level you can relate to what I have felt

I can't wait for this book to be published

I can't wait for my words to be your nightly read

I can't wait for my words to make you smile, wipe your tears, and help sew the scars of the pain you've felt

A final message...

There are many morals and lessons I want you to gain from this book. I want you to take strength from my loss, not pity. I didn't publish this to be treated like glass; I did this for anyone that needs the reminder that they are put on this Earth for a reason. Take it from me, this life is far too short to endure pain in silence. Seize every opportunity; do not let your fear control you; and love unconditionally. Make the best of this life; strive to be the best version of yourself. I have healed; I have moved on and buried my pain. I'm opening up more every day, trying to revive that hopeful girl that died all those years ago. Listen to your heart and never lose the best of yourself.

With love,

Zelda

ACKNOWLEDGEMENTS

There are so many names that come to mind when I think of who inspired me to write all I have felt.

Mom & Dad – Believing in me no matter what. I am so lucky. Most could only wish for such amazing parents like you.

Nonny & Grandpa – For inspiring me to start writing and for all the endless love.

Grandma – Teaching me kindness is something everyone deserves.

My family – Thank you for the consistent support. That is the reason I have the courage to chase anything my heart desires.

My supportive, amazing friends – Internet and in person friends, thank you for being my therapy, for helping me laugh when I so desperately needed it. Thank you for being my sunshine.

Poets everywhere – You are all my heroes. It takes guts to open your wounds in attempt to heal others.

Special thanks to Linda D. for editing this book!

ABOUT THE AUTHOR:

ZELDA BLACK is a twenty-year-old poet living in New York. She started writing poetry at a young age which eventually led to her publishing her first book. She is currently enrolled in college with hopes to pursue voice acting and film.

(ISBN 978-1-09835-506-7)

311